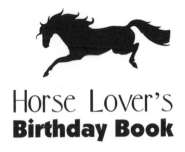

Horse Lover's
Birthday Book

This book belongs to:

_____

D1596271

I love horses!

It's better to give than receive!
—Photo contributed by Linda Huffstutler of Salem, IN

—Photo contributed by
Elizabeth Merril of Cape Porpoise, ME

I love horses!

Horse Lover's
Birthday Book

Written & compiled by June V. Evers

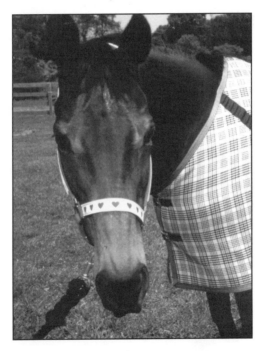

Published by Horse Hollow Press, Inc.

I love horses!

Dedicated to horses and all the humans who love them!

Thank you to all my favorite and patient tack stores — you *are* the best!

Thank you Jim Kersbergen and Blake Banta.

Cover photo: Miss Mattie Hayes, Paint horse, owned by Stacey Vigo.
Cover photo credit: Suzi Drnec of
Hobby Horse Clothing Company, Chino, CA.
Title page photo credit: Blake Banta of the
Curvon Corporation, makers of Baker Blankets.

MADE COMPLETELY IN THE U.S.A.

ISBN: 0-9638814-4-2

1st printing: November 2000

V.P. of Operations

Within these pages, record all of your important dates next to the corresponding month and day. You will never forget birthdays, anniversaries, engagements, foaling and new horse delivery dates ever again! This is one book that you will add to year after year. It will become a genuine keepsake. *Enjoy!*

Here are some tips to help keep your Birthday Book organized.

1 **Write birthdays in one color pen,** wedding anniversaries in another, etc. A quick glance will easily tell you what important event is coming up.

2 **Keep the Birthday Book in your purse** so when you hear of a new special date, you can write it down immediately. Then, no one will be forgotten.

3 **Transfer the names from this book to** your regular calendar or date book at the first of each month. Make a notation in your calendar a few weeks before the important date, allowing you time to buy or create a gift.

4 **Make a gift reminder note next to each** person's name in the address section. Jot down what you give them each year.

Poco —Photo contributed by Suzi Drnec, Hobby Horse Clothing Company of Chino, CA

Mary Ellen, the author's Thoroughbred

Cherokee —Photo contributed by Heather Joy Delong of Logan, OH

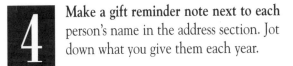

I love horses!

GIFT IDEAS:

1. **Grass Seed Cake:** With a lack of lush grass in the cold winter months, here is a treat that is a delight to give:
   - Plant grass seed or whole oats in a cake pan filled with top soil. Once the sprouts are 2 - 3 inches long, serve.
   - GARNISH SUGGESTION: Dribble on molasses and sliced apples.
     — *Contributed by Kristine Gunther of Dousman, WI*

Group hug! Cody T. Breeze adored by Aimée, Beth and Amanda.
—Photo contributed by Aimée LaPlante of Cazenovia, NY

Ollie By Gollie and Cheryl Ryan
—Photo contributed by Nina Lieberman, Whisper Wind Farm of Pine Island, NY

2. **Make a one-time donation to a local horse rescue:** Better yet, donate your time to help feed, groom and ride to speed adoptions.

3. **Sponsor a horse for a year at a retirement or rescue facility in your friend's name.** Here are some deserving agencies:
   - Standardbred Retirement
     PO Box 57
     Blairstown, NJ 07825
   - Thoroughbred Retirement
     1050 Hwy 35, Suite 351
     Shrewsbury, NJ 07702
   - Ryerss Farm for Aged Equines
     1710 Ridge Road
     Pottstown, PA 19465
   Check with your local tack store for rescue agencies in your area.

4. **Give a gift of labor!**
   Here are some ideas:
   - Winter: Shovel all the barn paths
   - Spring clean: Dust or shop-vac cobwebs and sweep the barn floor spotless
   - Summer: Baths for all the horses
   - Fall: Sheet and blanket cleaning
   - Major mucking: Completely strip and fill stalls with fresh bedding
   - The ultimate tack-cleaning

JANUARY

1. _____
2. _____
3. _____
4. _____
5. _____
6. _____
7. _____
8. _____
9. _____
10. _____
11. _____
12. _____
13. _____
14. _____
15. _____
16. _____
17. _____
18. _____
19. _____
20. _____
21. _____
22. _____
23. _____
24. _____
25. _____
26. _____
27. _____
28. _____
29. _____
30. _____
31. _____

GIFT IDEAS:

1. **Hide 'n Find birthday bale cake:**
Place a bale of hay in your horse's paddock. Clip the twine only, don't shake the bale apart. Insert carrots, apples and horse treats deep within the bale in different spots. Then, turn your horse out. He will enjoy tossing the bale around to find the treats hidden inside.

   - WARNING: Stay away from alfalfa, as it will be too rich if your horse is not accustomed to it. And, if there's more than one turned-out horse, don't expect them to share. Each horse *must* receive his own *Hide 'n Find Bale* or they will squabble over the goodies.

2. **Bouquets of carrots with long green tops:** Tie together with braided hay.

3. **A bouquet of the choicest pieces of hay tied together with long red licorice.**

4. **Bouquets of fresh dandelions.**
   — *Contributed by Adele Bailey, Fox Cry Farm of Conowingo, MD.*

5. **Anniversary treat du jour:** Place one sliced apple in a feed bucket, dribble with molasses and confectioners sugar.

6. **Tack cleaning gift basket:**
Fill an 8-quart bucket (the perfect size for tack cleaning!) with all the usual tack cleaning elements, such as: Saddle soap, conditioner and tack sponges. Also include: toothbrushes (for tough dirt), paint brushes (for oiling) and wash cloths (for wiping up).

   - SPECIAL SUGGESTION: Include a bar of the most delightful smelling human hand soap for afterwards.
   - AN EXTRA-SPECIAL SUGGESTION: Include a hand-made gift certificate offering yourself as a tack cleaner extraordinaire!
   - PARTY SUGGESTION: Gather friends for a tack cleaning party.

A moment together. Linda Boggs and Shiek of Eagle River, AK. —Photo contributed by Suzi Drnec, Hobby Horse Clothing of Chino, CA

FEBRUARY

1. _____
2. _____
3. _____
4. _____
5. _____
6. _____
7. _____
8. _____
9. _____
10. _____
11. _____
12. _____
13. _____
14. _____
15. _____
16. _____
17. _____
18. _____
19. _____
20. _____
21. _____
22. _____
23. _____
24. _____
25. _____
26. _____
27. _____
28. _____
29. _____

FEBRUARY

GIFT IDEAS:

1. **Tin of treats:** Use an antique tin or interesting container and simply fill it with store-bought or homemade treats. Visit garage sales or antique stores to find the perfect tin.

2. **Bucket O' Snaps:** Fill a tote with double-end, single-end and quick-release snaps. Include also any other snap that would fulfill a barn owner's wish list.
   — *Contributed by Linda Abrams, Pegasus Place School of Riding & Driving of Milner, GA*

3. **Macramé lead ropes, halters, cross-ties:** Use baling twine as string.
   - MACRAMÉ SUGGESTION: Braid in colored string to match barn colors.
     — *Contributed by Linda Abrams, Pegasus Place School of Riding & Driving of Milner, GA*

4. **A long celebratory grooming!**
   — *Contributed by Adrienne Bradley of Bethlehem, PA*

Itty, bitty mini fits under the Christmas tree. —Photo contributed by Boot & Lynn Ingles of Sorento, IL

5. **Long, luxurious birthday bubble baths** — for your horse, silly!

6. **Horse picture frames:** Make frames out of old horse shoes. Paint with bright colors or simply varnish. Then, tape the picture to the back of the shoe so the image shows through the front. Use a piece of wire and twist through top two holes to make a hanger.
   — *Contributed by Jody Phillips of Exton, PA*
   - SPECIAL SUGGESTION: Use ribbon threaded through the holes for a prettier hanger.
     — *Contributed by Ellen Taylor, Harness Horse Youth Foundation of Carmel, IN*

7. **Create a wind chime with old horseshoes.** With fishing line, tie horseshoes at various lengths to an interesting piece of driftwood.
   - "ARTY" SUGGESTION: In addition to the horseshoes, try tying bits, stirrups, stall name plates, any unique metal item from the barn to your wind chimes.
     — *Contributed by Katie Lynn Ortberg of Haymarket, VA*
   - ANOTHER "ARTY" SUGGESTION: Use the horseshoe itself instead of driftwood to secure your chimes.
     — *Contributed by Carrie Graves of Hayden Lake, ID*

MARCH

1. _____
2. _____
3. _____
4. _____
5. _____
6. _____
7. _____
8. _____
9. _____
10. _____
11. _____
12. _____
13. _____
14. _____
15. _____
16. _____
17. _____
18. _____
19. _____
20. _____
21. _____
22. _____
23. _____
24. _____
25. _____
26. _____
27. _____
28. _____
29. _____
30. _____
31. _____

MARCH

11

GIFT IDEAS:

1. **Decorative kitchen gifts:** Hand paint English or western stirrups to make unique napkin or letter holders.
   — *Contributed by Kathy Andrews, Hunter Cross Farm of Reidsville, NC*

2. **A basket of beauty:** Fill a new 5-gallon water bucket with equine bath supplies. Include: sponges, shampoos, conditioners, disposable razors (for horse whiskers), Listerine (for itchy spots), a new spray nozzle for the hose, the plushest terry-cloth towels, sweat scrapers, etc. Don't limit yourself to conventional items. Choose *luxurious* supplies that your recipient would never indulge in but would love.
   - EXTRA SUGGESTION: Include human bath supplies, too.

3. **Birthday trail rides:** Birthday hats for both horses and humans.
   — *Contributed by Mary Jane Ciraco of Deland, FL*

4. **Store-bought molasses cookies wrapped in colored cellophane and tied with a bow.** Surprise 'em and leave in the tack trunk!

5. **Peppermints!** Garnish your horse's evening meal with a few, just because.

6. **Future shade:** Plant a shade tree right next to the paddock in a sunny spot. It will grow into wonderful shade for the horses and, best of all, your friends will remember it for years to come.
   - WARNING: Be sure to stay clear of poisonous trees: Oak, Red Maple, Black Walnut, etc.

7. **Paddock surprise jubilee:** Hide carrots and apples throughout your horse's paddock for him to find as he leisurely grazes.

More presents for me? Of course!—Photo contributed by Linda Huffstutler of Salem, IN

Long sunset trail rides. Send invitations and invite everyone! —Photo contributed by Carole Walker of Chino, CA

APRIL

1. _____
2. _____
3. _____
4. _____
5. _____
6. _____
7. _____
8. _____
9. _____
10. _____
11. _____
12. _____
13. _____
14. _____
15. _____
16. _____
17. _____
18. _____
19. _____
20. _____
21. _____
22. _____
23. _____
24. _____
25. _____
26. _____
27. _____
28. _____
29. _____
30. _____

GIFT IDEAS:

1. **A matching set:** Purchase matching wraps, a saddle pad and a polo shirt (for human). Or even, *make* a matching saddle pad.
   — *Contributed by Adele Bailey,*
   Fox Cry Farm of Conowingo, MD

2. **Hire a masseuse ...** Surprise them with a massage for both horse and rider.

3. **Birthday Bundt:** Mix sweet feed, bran and molasses to make a very thick paste. Press into a bundt cake pan and refrigerate for 1 hour. Turn over on a flat pan and serve.
   - GARNISH: Grate a carrot over the cake and sprinkle with confectioners sugar.

Party idea: Be a bum for a day and let your horse be a horse. —Contributed by Mary Jane Ciraco of Deland, FL. Pictured: 27-year-old Dulcie enjoying his "Be a Bum for a Day!" with a roll in the shavings. —Photo contributed by Bonnie Scribner, Balance Farm of Mineral, VA

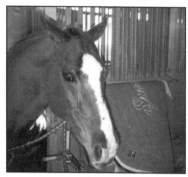

Sparky and his matching blanket, stall guard, sheet, halter ... everything! —Photo contributed by Anita Cantor of Scottsdale, AZ

4. **Simple bloomin' treat:** Shake the blooms from a flake of alfalfa hay into a feed bucket, stir in sliced apples, and top with a bit of sweet feed.

5. **Horse show checklist:** Create a packing list of everything needed for successful showing. Laminate it so it can be wiped clean after each use.
   - EXTRA SUGGESTION: Include a photo album as part of the gift to record photos of future wins.
   — *Contributed by Shirley Gough Gentry of Lexington, KY*

6. **New trailer welcome wagon:** Create a trailer tool box that includes a first aid kit for humans and horses, horse show grooming aids, tire gauge, flashlight with batteries, Wash 'n Dries and a small amount of "mad" money in a plastic bag.
   — *Contributed by Diane Nafis of Laurel Springs, NJ*

MAY

1. _____
2. _____
3. _____
4. _____
5. _____
6. _____
7. _____
8. _____
9. _____
10. _____
11. _____
12. _____
13. _____
14. _____
15. _____
16. _____
17. _____
18. _____
19. _____
20. _____
21. _____
22. _____
23. _____
24. _____
25. _____
26. _____
27. _____
28. _____
29. _____
30. _____
31. _____

M A Y

GIFT IDEAS:

1. **A special grazing:** Let your horse "mow" away on a lawn that's too long!
   - REMEMBER: Horses not accustomed to lush grass should only graze for short periods and never, never let your horse eat grass clippings.

2. **Homemade treats served on a silver tray:** Check out *The Original Book of Horse Treats* (a cookbook with recipes) for some unique ideas.

3. **Wall hangings:** Attach dried flowers, old fashioned buttons and other interesting items onto horse shoes with a hot glue gun. String a matching ribbon through nail holes. Reinforce at the holes with hot glue.
   — Contributed by Denise Reynolds of Elizabeth, PA
   - EXTRA-SPECIAL SUGGESTION: Check craft stores and garage sales for unique items to glue onto shoes.
   - ANOTHER SUGGESTION: Paint on WELCOME for front doors.
   - ANTIQUE LOVERS: Find old, old horse shoes at barn sales.
   - WARNING: Hot glue guns will get hot, be very careful!

4. **Customed designed halter:** Using any color nylon halter, paint a thin layer of fabric paint over the nose and cheek pieces. Sprinkle on glitter and sequins. Let dry.
   — Contributed by Denise Reynolds of Elizabeth, PA
   - EXTRA-SPECIAL SUGGESTION: When dry, add polka dots of fabric paint for some splash!

Foal showers! A great way to get together. And, don't forget the gifts. —Photo contributed by Linda Huffstutter of Salem, IN

A June bride! When Shirley and Charlie got married, 22-year-old Griffin joined them down the aisle. Note, the bridle is made of strung pearls crossing over the nose with macraméd cheek and brow bands. —Photo contributed by Shirley Gough Gentry of Lexington, KY

JUNE

1. _____
2. _____
3. _____
4. _____
5. _____
6. _____
7. _____
8. _____
9. _____
10. _____
11. _____
12. _____
13. _____
14. _____
15. _____
16. _____
17. _____
18. _____
19. _____
20. _____
21. _____
22. _____
23. _____
24. _____
25. _____
26. _____
27. _____
28. _____
29. _____
30. _____

JUNE

GIFT IDEAS:

1. **Bucket full of warmth:** Fill a water bucket with new terry cloth towels, wash cloths, sponges (both tack and body), paper towels, handy wipes, etc.
   - EXTRA SUGGESTION: Include extra wash cloths, as they are wonderful for wiping faces, cleaning gooey noses and applying fly spray.

2. **Plastic horse wardrobe kit:** The idea of this gift is to provide a child with one or two plastic horses and *all* the material to create their own horse clothing, such as saddles, bridles, blankets and leg wraps. In a storage container, place 1 or 2 plastic horses, assorted fabrics, brown felt (for the saddle and bridle), needle and thread, scissors, tape and glue.
   - WARNING: This gift should be intended for children who can handle scissors and sewing safely.

3. **The horse lover's trellis:** Weld horse shoes together in a unique pattern. Then weld an old rasp at the bottom to make the ground stake. For experienced welders only!
   — *Contributed by Ellen Taylor, Harness Horse Youth Foundation of Carmel, IN She says it looks great with honey suckle, clematis or roses. Plant each variety for a trellis bouquet.*

Cody, an 11-year-old Morgan, striking a pose and smiling for the camera. —Photo contributed by Liz Dunshee of Marlborough, CT

Gypsy hamming it up! —Photo contributed by Holly Abbot of Crescent City, FL

Nothing beats a tray of delectable treats … especially when they are served on a silver platter. —Photo contributed by Patricia Noonan of Naperville, IL

JULY

1. _____
2. _____
3. _____
4. _____
5. _____
6. _____
7. _____
8. _____
9. _____
10. _____
11. _____
12. _____
13. _____
14. _____
15. _____
16. _____
17. _____
18. _____
19. _____
20. _____
21. _____
22. _____
23. _____
24. _____
25. _____
26. _____
27. _____
28. _____
29. _____
30. _____
31. _____

JULY

GIFT IDEAS:

1. **Subscriptions to horse magazines!**

2. **Gift certificates to your local tack store.** Get creative with the gift wrap and packaging. See page 30 for ideas.

3. **Gift certificate for 10 riding, driving or training sessions.**

4. **Big basket of treats:** Fill a feed tub with a taste-testing bag of various brands of horse treats.

5. **"No hoof, no horse" gift basket:** Purchase a grooming tote and fill it with all sorts of hoof creams, oils and packing supplies as well as several styles of hoof picks.

6. **Make jump standards and brightly painted jump poles!**
   — *Contributed by Nina Lieberman, Whisper Winds Farm of Pine Island, NY. She received a set from her father and brother as a wedding present.*

7. **Off to school knapsack gift basket:** Purchase pencils, pens, notepads, spiral notebooks, insulated lunch bags and folders — all with horses on them.
   - SPECIAL SUGGESTION: Use fabric paint to personalize a blank totebag (paint and totebags are available at most craft stores.)

—Photo contributed by Heather Zawisiak of Branchville, NJ with 4-year-old rescued Quarter Horse mare Leah

—Photo contributed by Barbara Mannis of Malvern, PA with Sky's the Limit. Barbara is co-author of The Incredible Little Book of 10,001 Names for Horses.
—Photo by Gallop Prints

Wiping the lipstick off after a big smooch on the nose! —Photo contributed by Patricia Noonan of Naperville, IL with 20-year-old Crescent. She says, "They deserve every bit of lovin' they get!"—Photo by Jamie Wilson of Warrenville, IL

AUGUST

1. _____
2. _____
3. _____
4. _____
5. _____
6. _____
7. _____
8. _____
9. _____
10. _____
11. _____
12. _____
13. _____
14. _____
15. _____
16. _____
17. _____
18. _____
19. _____
20. _____
21. _____
22. _____
23. _____
24. _____
25. _____
26. _____
27. _____
28. _____
29. _____
30. _____
31. _____

AUGUST

GIFT IDEAS:

1. **Seasonal photo essay of the farm:** Frame the photos side by side to coincide with the seasons.
   — *Contributed by Nina Lieberman, Whisper Winds Farm of Pine Island, NY*

2. **Favorite photo mousepad:** Simply have a favorite photo made into a sweatshirt, t-shirt or even a mousepad.
   — *Contributed by Linda Pontnack of Winchester, IL*

3. **Hire a photographer for "glam" shots of both horse and human:**
   - EXTRA-SPECIAL SUGGESTION: Design and make period costumes for horse and rider to wear, such as: Medieval, Victorian or even Eqyptian!
   - TIME-SAVING SUGGESTION: Try a costume or party store for the basics, then customize each costume with costume jewelry.
   - MONEY-SAVING SUGGESTION: Garage sales, thrift stores and Salvation Army stores are wonderful places to find inexpensive outfits and jewelry that you can incorporate into your costume.
   - PARTY SUGGESTION: Turn the photo session into a party that no one will ever forget!

Planning a horse show?
Unconventional gifts are great for horse shows!
—Photo contributed by Leah Yurasek of Farmington Hills, MI

What a photo-op! —Photo contributed by Janice Elsishans of Oak Ridge, NJ. Janice swears by thrift stores for costuming. And she thinks creatively by using an upside-down Easter basket wrapped with fabric as a bonnet. A+ for creativity here! (When using an umbrella, accustom your horse to it slowly.)

SEPTEMBER

1. _____
2. _____
3. _____
4. _____
5. _____
6. _____
7. _____
8. _____
9. _____
10. _____
11. _____
12. _____
13. _____
14. _____
15. _____
16. _____
17. _____
18. _____
19. _____
20. _____
21. _____
22. _____
23. _____
24. _____
25. _____
26. _____
27. _____
28. _____
29. _____
30. _____

SEPTEMBER

GIFT IDEAS:

1. **Treat your horse to sun bath!**
   — *Contributed by Amy Van Allsburg of Glendale, AZ*
   - EXTRA-SPECIAL SUGGESTION: On a warm winter day, remove your horse's blankets and hang them inside out to warm in the sun. While outside, groom your horse, then, place the now snugly warm blankets on your horse.

Sunridge Wrangler, a blue-eyed dun Appaloosa. A horse with this lovely color combination "makes a great gift!" —Photo contributed by Klaudya Callender, Sunridge Ranch of Arcadia, LA

New horse blankets or certificates to wash and repair old ones

2. **Quickie cake:** Bake a box-mix carrot cake. Mix molasses and crimped oats together for icing.
   - GARNISH SUGGESTION: Peel a carrot and lay the "curls" over the top.
   — *Contributed by Nanci Falley, American Indian Horse Registry of Lockart, TX. She also serves this recipe to humans who usually comment on the oats.*
   - SPECIAL SUGGESTION: Use the tiny muffin tins to make bite-sized treats.

3. **Mail boxes:** You can make your own horse head mailbox starting with an inexpensive plastic one. First, draw a horse head onto plywood, then, cut it out with a jigsaw. Screw the horse head to the top of the mail box. Paint the box and the wooden horse head with your favorite horse colors — appaloosa, chestnut or paint! When both are dry, drill a hole in the back of the box and pull some real horse hair through to make a tail. Tape it to the inside of the box.
   — *Contributed by Orlando Fasano, Rolling Rock Ranch of Centerreach, NY*
   - WARNING: If you are not familiar with power tools, be sure to have a parent or a carpenter help you.

What a wonderful gift for a riding or boarding stable!

OCTOBER

1. _____
2. _____
3. _____
4. _____
5. _____
6. _____
7. _____
8. _____
9. _____
10. _____
11. _____
12. _____
13. _____
14. _____
15. _____
16. _____
17. _____
18. _____
19. _____
20. _____
21. _____
22. _____
23. _____
24. _____
25. _____
26. _____
27. _____
28. _____
29. _____
30. _____
31. _____

OCTOBER

GIFT IDEAS:

1. **Keep 'em shining grooming box:** Pick up an unpainted wooden box from a craft store. Customize the outside of the box with acrylic paints, magic markers, etc. Paint hearts, horses, stars or whatever you like all over the box. Include the owner's and horse's names, etc. Once dry, literally stuff the box with horse brushes.

2. **Extra special holiday treatment:** Cross-tie your horse. Dampen a towel with warm (not hot) water. Drape the warm towel over your horse's face. Let it sit for a few minutes, like a warm facial. Then, remove by wiping the horse's entire face. Use a clean dry towel and gently dry, careful to rub every itchy spot!
   — *Contributed by Paree Hecht of Commack, NY*
   - SPECIAL SUGGESTION: Plan a day where the horses receive facials and so do you!

3. **Horse books:** *The Original Book of Horse Treats, The Ultimate Guide to Pampering Your Horse* and *The Incredible Little Book of 10,001 Names for Horses,* published by Horse Hollow Press.

4. **Scrapbook memories:** Place photos in the first few pages of a scrapbook to start a lifetime of memories.
   - SPECIAL SUGGESTION: You can make your own scrapbook with a 3-ring binder and plastic sheet covers for presentations. Decorate the cover with metallic markers, etc.
   - EXTRA-SPECIAL SUGGESTION: Play photographer for the summer! Secretly photograph the gift recipient throughout the show season. Show all the ups and downs, capture the warm and fuzzy moments, save ticket stubs, programs, etc. Place them all chronologically into the notebook. Personalize the cover with a title, such as: *Rebecca's & Misty's 2001 Show Season Adventure.* Sign your name and add a heartfelt message inside.

Hugs and kisses for Allie Girl from Katie.
—*Photo contributed by Katie Citelli of Goshen, NY*

NOVEMBER

1. _____
2. _____
3. _____
4. _____
5. _____
6. _____
7. _____
8. _____
9. _____
10. _____
11. _____
12. _____
13. _____
14. _____
15. _____
16. _____
17. _____
18. _____
19. _____
20. _____
21. _____
22. _____
23. _____
24. _____
25. _____
26. _____
27. _____
28. _____
29. _____
30. _____

NOVEMBER

GIFT IDEAS:

1. **Christmas stockings:** Hang one on every stall door stuffed with treats and out of your horse's reach.

   — *Contributed by Adele Bailey, Fox Cry Farm of Conowingo, MD*

   - SPECIAL SUGGESTION: Sew your own stockings. Use unconventional fabrics, such as plaid, striped or hot green and fake zebra fur for trim! Write names in glue and sprinkle with sparkles.

   — *Contributed by Marcy Gamester of Westford, MA. She made an adorable stocking for Mary Ellen, the author's horse.*

   - STOCKING STUFFER SUGGESTIONS: Alfalfa cubes, peppermints, candy canes, double-end snaps, curry combs and brushes, carrots and apples, homemade or store-bought horse treats.

2. **Braided horse hair ornaments:** Make a small circle of braided horse hair. Tie it together with wire and make a loop for hanging. Use a hot-glue gun to add stars or sequins.

   — *Contributed by Sandy Larkin, Shanadar Arabians of Webster, NY*

3. **Wreaths of red and green:** Select seven red and seven green apples. Arrange them in alternating colors. Pierce each apple with a straightened coat hanger. Fashion the wire loaded with fruit in a circle and twist the excess into a knot at the top. Cut off extra wire and wrap with duct tape to cover sharp edges, then add a large red bow.

   — *Contributed by Jackie Hahn-Winans of Northridge, CA. She says it makes a wonderful decoration and treat!*

   - WARNING: Feed only during your supervision.

—*Photo contributed by Rosemary Speakes, Blue Haven Farm of West Milton, OH. Everyone at her farm, horses and humans, receive stockings.*

Dress as Santa and dispense treats to everyone along your trail ride. Bring along friends for a whole entourage of gift-giving Santas! —Contributed by Bernice Duquay of Fredericton, Canada. —Photo contributed by Eloise King of Pineland, FL

DECEMBER

1. _____
2. _____
3. _____
4. _____
5. _____
6. _____
7. _____
8. _____
9. _____
10. _____
11. _____
12. _____
13. _____
14. _____
15. _____
16. _____
17. _____
18. _____
19. _____
20. _____
21. _____
22. _____
23. _____
24. _____
25. _____
26. _____
27. _____
28. _____
29. _____
30. _____
31. _____

D E C E M B E R

WRAPPING SUGGESTIONS:

Innovative gift wrapping can be as much fun as creating the actual gift and it is a tremendous delight to the recipient that you took the time to *present* their *present* so well.

1. Insert a gift into a clean burlap bag. Braid baling twine together with red and green ribbons and use it to tie open end shut.

2. Fill a festive shopping bag with clean straw and add gift.

3. Place items in a decorative basket, feed or water bucket. Or use one of those cute 8-quart buckets available at your tack store.

4. Enclose a gift certificate in a brand new large-sized tack box! Or if you're handy, make a tack box.

5. Wrap with simple brown paper and cover it completely with horsey stickers and bumperstickers.

You'll never go wrong with homemade horse treats! Wrap in colored cellophane and top with a bow. —Photo contributed by Ashley Evans of Aberdeen, SD. Ashley won 1st prize at a 4-H baking contest with a recipe from The Original Book of Horse Treats.

The sound of music! —Photo contributed by Kristine Gunter, Mystic Meadows Farm of Dousman, WI. Windmere Mystic Lady, left, and Barbara's Blaze, right, are playing a battery-operated keyboard.

Danka, a 10-year-old Quarter Horse, leaping for joy. —Photo contributed by Lisa Miller of Corrales, NM

6. Dribble glue over plain brown paper and sprinkle on sparkles, oats or whatever you'd like. *Let gift dry completely.*

7. Use a rubber stamp or stencil to decorate brown or white butcher paper. Use a metallic marker to write messages, famous horse's names and breeds, etc. right onto the paper.

8. Try fabric as wrapping paper (fake fur is the most fun!) Use a glue gun (careful, they get hot!) to adhere sides and use braided baling twine as the ribbon.

9. Wrap with aluminum foil and secure with an old stirrup leather.

9. Use the daily racing newspaper as gift wrap. Cut a feed bag into strips and tape it end to end and tie into a bow.

10. Wrap Saran wrap around a package or feed bucket and tie into a beautiful bow. Dribble on glue and sprinkle with sparkles and sequins.

11. Take advantage of inexpensive paper tablecloths to wrap large gifts.

12. Cover a box with old horse show programs or photocopies of win pictures. Tie shut with a red satin ribbon.

Toys, toys, toys!—Photo contributed by Gaye Eck, Eck Quarter Horses of Manassas, VA

C-Star —Photo contributed by Carrie Graves of Hayden Lake, ID

YOUR IDEAS

Jot down your own creative ideas for future gift-giving!

IDEAS

YOUR IDEAS

ADDRESSES *(both horses & human!)*

A

B

C

D

E

G

F

H

I just love my horse!

I

K

J

L

I just love my horse!

M

O

N

P

I just love my horse!

Q

_____
_____
_____
_____
_____
_____
_____
_____
_____
_____
_____
_____
_____
_____

S

_____
_____
_____
_____
_____
_____
_____
_____
_____
_____
_____
_____
_____
_____

R

_____
_____
_____
_____
_____
_____
_____
_____
_____
_____
_____
_____
_____
_____

T

_____
_____
_____
_____
_____
_____
_____
_____
_____
_____
_____
_____
_____
_____

I just love my horse!

U

W

V

XYZ

I just love my horse!

WRITE US!

♥ **Look for other Horse Hollow Press books** at your local tack store: *The Original Book of Horse Treats* (a cookbook of horse treats), *The Ultimate Guide to Pampering Your Horse* (contains hundreds of handy hints) and *The Incredible Little Book of 10,001 Names for Horses* (a listing of literally thousands of names).

♥ **Be included in our other books:** Do you have any recipes, creative gift-making ideas, grooming tips or handy hints, home remedies, or just comments you'd like to share? Drop us a note, we might use it in an upcoming book!

♥ **Send along funny pictures** of your horse that we can use in upcoming books and newsletters.

♥ **Want to drop a note to the author?** Send it to June V. Evers at the address below.

♥ **Write for our free catalog** of products and books for horse lovers.

HORSE HOLLOW PRESS, Inc.
P.O. Box 456
Goshen, NY 10924-0456
www.horsehollowpress.com
E-mail: info@horsehollowpress.com

40

To order more copies, photocopy this page and mail to the address below. Or, visit your favorite tack or feed store!

Yes! Please send me [qty.] ____ copy(ies) of **HORSE LOVER'S BIRTHDAY BOOK** at $4.95 each.

And, I want your other books as well!
❑ Please send me [qty.] ____ copy(ies) of *The Incredible Little Book of 10,001 Names for Horses*, a book of literally thousands of horse names, at $8.95 each.
❑ And, send me [qty.] ____ copy(ies) of *The Ultimate Guide to Pampering Your Horse*, including hundreds of handy hints and pampering tips for people who love their horses, at $24.95 each.
❑ And, I would like [qty.] ____ copy(ies) of *The Original Book of Horse Treats*, a cookbook of recipes for treats and things I can make at home for my horse, at $19.95 each.
I have included $4.50 for shipping & packing. (Only $4.50 no matter how many books you order.)
Total enclosed: $_____ (Check, MO, or credit cards)

Mail to: HORSE HOLLOW PRESS
P.O. Box 456
Goshen, NY 10924-0456
OR CALL TOLL-FREE: 1-800-4-1-HORSE to order!

Name: _____
Address: _____
City/State/Zip: _____
Phone: _____
Visa/MC/AMEX: _____
Exp. Date: _____
Signature: _____